MY GRANDMA LIKES TO SAY

By DENISE BRENNAN-NELSON

Illustrated by JANE MONROE DONOVAN

To Grandma Carol—
Who is always there rain or shine
and is never a stick in the mud.

And in memory of Grandma Gerrie:
Life is short. Eat dessert first.

Denise

To Rylee, Levi, and Joelle Price who, as models, were fine as frogs hair *and*
as cute as bugs in a rug. *I had a* whale of a good time *working with you!*

Good things come in small packages *which describes my Grandma Alberta Dowty,*
who always had a heart of gold. *Thank you for your love and support.*

Jane

Sleeping Bear Press™

310 North Main Street, Suite 300
Chelsea, MI 48118
www.sleepingbearpress.com

THOMSON
★
GALE

© 2007 Thomson Gale, a part of the Thomson Corporation.

Thomson, Star Logo and Sleeping Bear Press are trademarks
and Gale is a registered trademark used herein under license.

Printed and bound in Canada.

First Edition

10 9 8 7 6 5 4 3 2 1

Library of Congress Cataloging-in-Publication Data

Brennan-Nelson, Denise.
My grandma likes to say / written by Denise Brennan-Nelson;
illustrated by Jane Monroe Donovan.
p. cm.
Summary: "Proverbs, clichés, and idioms are introduced in rhyme and illustrated
as a young child's literal interpretation. Each expression includes information
about its origin and original meaning"—Provided by publisher.
ISBN-13: 978-158536-284-4
ISBN-10: 1-58536-284-0
1. English language—Idioms—Juvenile literature. 2. Figures of speech—Juvenile
literature. 3. Proverbs, English—Juvenile literature. 4. Clichés—Juvenile literature.
I. Donovan, Jane Monroe, ill. II. Title.

PE1460.B725 2007
398.9'21—dc22   2006026002

Introduction

"Heavens to Betsy!" my grandma used to say, and I'd wonder, *Who's Betsy*? When she'd tell me I was *cute as a bug's ear*, I'd think, "Grandma must not like me very much." Bunnies and puppies are cute, but bugs' ears?!

Grandma liked to say, "She's not playing with a full deck." (I can't tell you who she was talking about. She told me not to *spill the beans*.) Every year on my birthday, Grandma gave me a silver dollar and advised me to *save it for a rainy day*.

And in Grandma's eyes *I hung the moon*.

I didn't always understand what Grandma meant but her strange expressions stirred my imagination. What funny pictures I created in my head!

What special expressions does *your* grandma use?

Listen to your grandma. She *wasn't born yesterday* and her words hold wisdom that comes from having *been around the block a few times*.

The bottom line is grandmas are in *a league all their own*. They *spoil us rotten*, teach us to *look for the silver lining in every cloud*, and encourage us to *follow our hearts*.

And *when push comes to shove* grandmas would *move heaven and earth* for us.

Does your grandma ever say things
you think are quite amusing?
Do they make you scratch your head?
Are her words a bit confusing?

My grandma says some funny things:
You're "wet behind the ears."
"Don't let the cat out of the bag."
And, "Are those crocodile tears?"

It seems to me my grandma
has a language all her own.
The other day I heard her say,
she'd "wait 'til the cows come home."

This has me a little worried.
Is she "coming apart at the seams?"
My grandma doesn't own a cow
but I won't "spill the beans."

When she tucks me in she whispers,
"You're as snug as a bug in a rug."
She gives me "butterfly kisses"
and wraps me in a "bear hug."

You'd really like my grandma.
They say she "broke the mold."
She's the "salt of the Earth," the "real McCoy"
and she has a "heart of gold."

The phrase "crocodile tears" comes from the ancient story that crocodiles make weeping sounds to lure their prey closer and cry while devouring their victims. Crocodiles do produce a tear-like fluid, but it is a myth that they weep with sorrow while gobbling their prey.

If someone says your tears are "crocodile tears," she means they are phony and your weeping is insincere.

Crocodiles store fat in their tails, so if it must, a crocodile can survive a long time without food—up to two years if it is a large adult. After so long without a meal, it would be understandable if the crocodile wept with relief and gratitude when a snack finally happened along!

If you've ever blabbed a secret, you've "spilled the beans." (You've also "let the cat out of the bag.") Ooops! "Keep it under your hat next time." These "spilled beans" can't be swept up with a broom and a dustpan. One theory about the origin of this expression goes back to ancient Greece where voters cast ballots with beans. A white bean dropped into a jar or upturned helmet was a "yes" vote, and a black bean was a "no." These edible votes were supposed to be secret, but occasionally someone accidentally or purposely knocked over the jar and spilled the beans, and the secret was out in plain sight.

"You're 'bright-eyed and bushy-tailed',"

my grandma likes to say.
I'm not sure what she means
but I like it anyway.

My brother often picks on me.
He likes to see me wail.
I can't seem to make him stop
until I lift my tail.

This expression means you look cheerful and lively, ready and eager to do something. It became popular in the United States and Canada about 50 years ago. Many people think a squirrel's tail was the inspiration behind it.

Tails are a very unique trait of an animal. Think about all the different types there are and what they can be used for.

If you ever see a skunk lift its tail, RUN!

I like looking "bright-eyed and bushy-tailed." How about you?

"You're 'growing like a weed,'"

my grandma likes to say.
I'm not sure what she means
but I like it anyway.

The weeds in Grandma's garden
grow bigger every day.
Most weeds are pesky problems
but weeds like me should stay.

If your grandma tells you that you are "growing like a weed" she means you are growing very fast. She would be more likely to say this if she hadn't seen you in awhile and is surprised at how much you have grown.

Do you ever help your grandma weed her garden? Some weeds come out with a tug. Others have such deep roots that you may need a shovel.

When I was a little girl, I picked the dandelions that dotted our lawn and proudly presented small bouquets to my momma. Now that I'm older I think of them as weeds. Why is that?

"Beware of a wolf in sheep's clothing,"

my grandma likes to say.
I'm not sure what she means
but I like it anyway.

If I were a wolf I would not want
a hot wooly suit to wear.
No curly locks or hooves for me.
I'd much rather run around bare.

This means that appearances can be deceptive. "Don't judge a book by its cover," is another idiom that reminds us not to judge someone or something by appearances.

Sheep are considered gentle, while wolves have the reputation of being dangerous. If a wolf wanted to trick you into thinking he was harmless, he might disguise himself as a sheep. People can do this, too. They can disguise who they are and what they want.

This saying is in one of Aesop's fables and also in the Bible (Matthew 7:15).

Can you think of stories with a sneaky wolf?

If you're having a conversation and you bring up an unrelated idea or topic, someone may say, "That's a horse of a different color."

When a horse is born, it is registered and that registration includes a record of its hair color. If the horse is sold and its color doesn't match the color on the registration, some would think it was a different horse.

In the *Wizard of Oz*, Dorothy rides around the Emerald City in a horse-drawn buggy. The horse pulling the buggy keeps changing colors. When Dorothy inquires about it, she is told it is a "horse of a different color."

William Shakespeare used a similar phrase in his play *Twelfth Night*, written in 1601.

I once owned a purple, polka-dotted pony … but "that's a horse of a different color."

"That's a horse of a different color,"

my grandma likes to say.
I'm not sure what she means
but I like it anyway.

Polka dots and stripes,
purple, orange, and blue—
What color would a horse be
if it were up to YOU?

If you are waiting for something to happen that never will, like your brother turning into a frog or your favorite teddy bear coming alive, you could say, "when pigs fly."

"When pigs fly,"

my grandma likes to say.
I'm not sure what she means
but I like it anyway.

His ears are pink and pointy.
His nose seems rather BIG.
Now I know the reason why—
My pilot is a PIG!

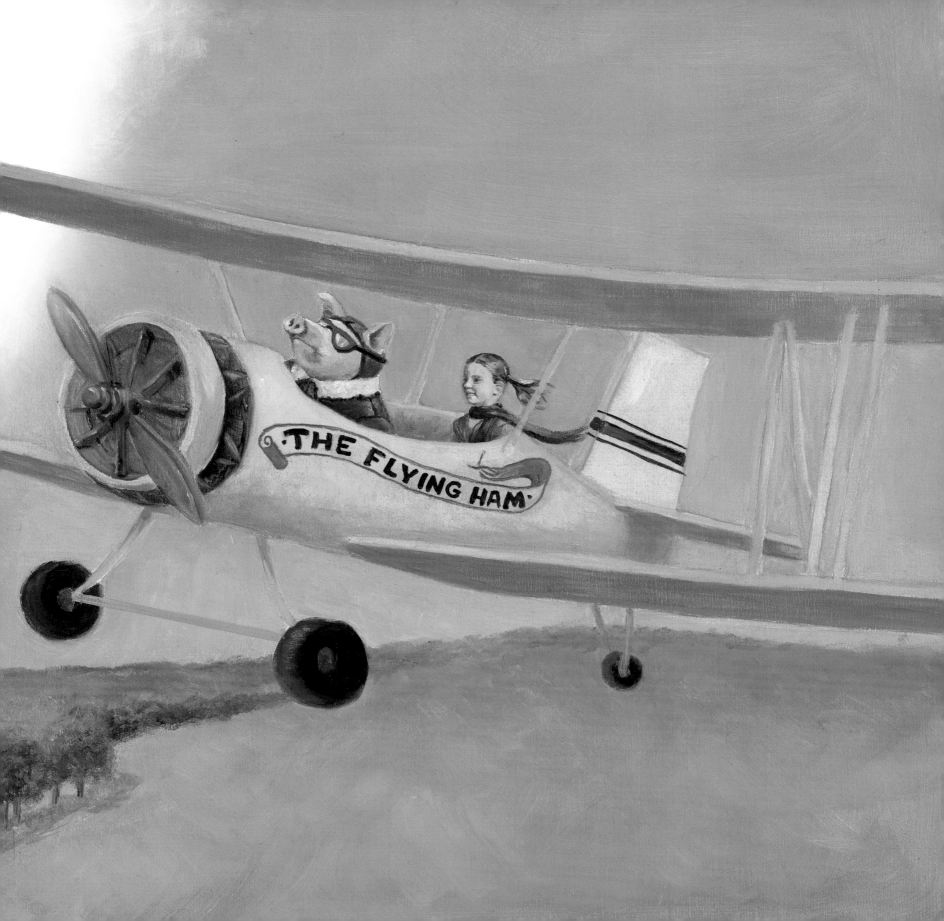

"When the cat's away the mice will play"

my grandma likes to say.
I'm not sure what she means
but I like it anyway.

Baseball, soccer, video games—
Mice play them all!
Nets and pucks and hockey sticks
and hoops for basketball.

This expression has been around since the 1600s and appears in many languages. It means that when someone in authority such as a parent, teacher, or boss (the cat) is not around, those being supervised (the mice) will play. What do you do when the "cat" is away?

I grew up in an old farmhouse that we occasionally shared with mice. When I squealed and jumped my parents told me, "Mice are more afraid of you than you are of them." I didn't believe it then, and I still don't!

Do cats and mice ever play together?

Have you ever broken something because you were careless or clumsy? If so, you might have been told, "You're like a bull in a china shop."

A bull charging through a store, knocking everything over would cause quite a scene, don't you think?

One of Aesop's fables is about a donkey in a potter's shop. Do you think a donkey or a bull would do more damage?

Ask your grandma if she has china and, if so, ask her to tell you about it.

CHINA SHOPPE & TEA ROOM

"Like a bull in a china shop,"

my grandma likes to say.
I'm not sure what she means
but I like it anyway.

I sat with a bull in a china shop
sipping dainty cups of tea.
He ordered a blueberry muffin
and a cranberry scone for me.

China
Shoppe
&
Tea
Room

"I'm no 'spring chicken'!"

my grandma likes to say.
I'm not sure what she means
but I like it anyway.

I know she's not a chicken!
Grandma can't lay eggs.
But wouldn't it be funny
if she had springs for legs?

Chicks usually hatch in the spring so a "spring chicken" is young.

If your grandma uses this expression, which was recorded as early as 1711, she means she isn't young anymore and may not have the energy she once had. You can tell her it doesn't matter because she is "young at heart."

There are many expressions that include chickens: "Feather your nest"; "Fly the coop"; "Don't put all your eggs in one basket"; "Chicken feed"; "Chickens come home to roost"; and "Don't count your chickens before they hatch." Can you think of any others?

If you were "knee-high to a grasshopper," how tall would you be? What would you be able to do that you can't do at your current height?

In 1814 you may have heard someone say "knee-high" to a toad, a mosquito, and even a bumblebee. It wasn't until 1850 that grasshopper caught on, most likely because grasshoppers do have knees. Their knee joints are where their energy is stored and are what allows them to jump so high.

If you ever meet a giant grasshopper, ask him to take you for a ride.

P.S. Don't forget to eat your vegetables!

"Knee-high to a grasshopper,"

my grandma likes to say.
I'm not sure what she means
but I like it anyway.

I bumped into a grasshopper;
I only reached his knees.
I asked him how he grew so tall.
He said, "I ate my peas."

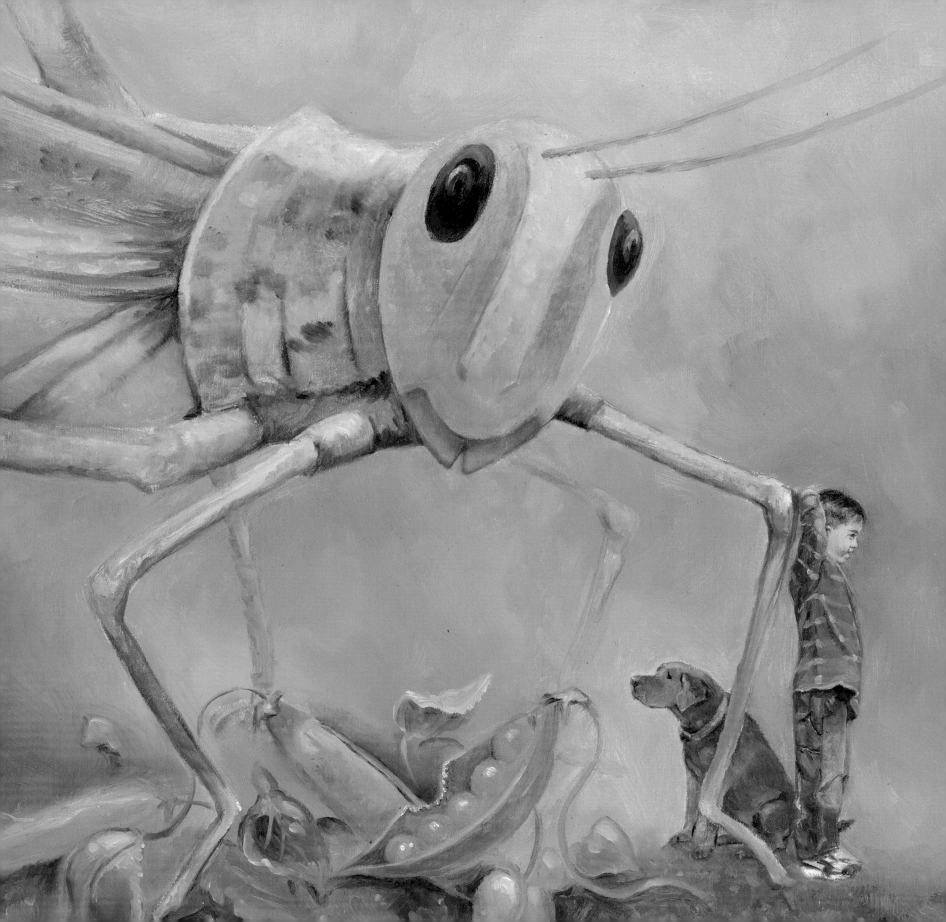

"Everything's coming up roses,"

my grandma likes to say.
I'm not sure what she means
but I like it anyway.

They started in the garden,
but now they're everywhere!
They're in my bath and in my bed
and in my underwear!

This expression means life is good. "Life is a bed of roses" has a similar meaning. Personally, I wouldn't want to sleep on a bed of thorny roses, would you? Ouch!

Roses have been symbols of love and beauty for centuries. There are more than 100 species of wild roses and they come in many colors, including black and blue. Different colored roses have different meanings. For instance, the red rose symbolizes love, white symbolizes innocence and secrecy, and yellow symbolizes friendship. If you want to send me roses, I'll take one of each color.

One more thing ... "Take time to smell the roses!"

"Hit the hay" means it is
time to go to bed.

Mattresses used to be stuffed with hay or straw, so
when someone was going to bed he was "hitting the hay."
He may have been sharing his bed with bugs living in the straw,
which is where the saying "don't let the bed bugs bite" originated.

Some think that this expression came from wanderers in the 1930s who
traveled around the country doing odd jobs. At night they slept on a pile of
hay in a field, or if they were lucky, in a barn.

What is the mattress that you sleep on stuffed with? Air, water, feathers?

"Hit the hay,"

my grandma likes to say.
I'm not sure what she means
but I like it anyway.

My grandma gives me good advice.
She tells me not to fight.
Then why does Grandma "hit the hay"
every single night?

I really love my grandma
and the things she likes to say:
"Carpe diem!", "C'est la vie!" and

"Where there's a will there's a way."

But of all the things my grandma says
my favorite has to be:
"'Rules are made to be broken'
when you come and stay with me."

Carpe diem is Latin and means "Seize the day!"
C'est la vie is French for "That's life."

Food for Thought

Rome was not built in a day and neither was the English language. There are thousands of idioms in the English language and many have been around for centuries.

Sometimes idioms can be confusing but they can also be fun! Don't let them go *in one ear and out the other*. See if you can find the "hidden" meaning in them.

Here are a few more idioms to *wet your whistle*.

That's the way the ball bounces is said when something happens in life that you can't do anything about. It means that life is just that way. *That's the way the cookie crumbles* has a similar meaning.

It is a *blessing in disguise* when something unfavorable turns out to be good.

In one ear and out the other means that you are not listening to or hearing what is being said.

If you *put your foot in your mouth*, you said something that you shouldn't have.

Barking up the wrong tree means to choose the wrong course of action.

When you are *as mad as a wet hen* you are extremely angry.

If something is *as clean as a whistle* it is spotless.

Leave no stone unturned means to be thorough and do everything you can to carry out a task.

If you are *footloose and fancy-free* you are not tied to a certain person, place, or job.

You can catch more flies with honey than vinegar Means more can be accomplished by being pleasant than disagreeable.

If you *hitch your wagon to a star* you are aiming high to reach a goal.

We'll cross that bridge when we come to it means not to worry about what might happen in the future.

When you *get up on the wrong side of the bed* you are in a bad or grouchy mood.

People who live in glass houses shouldn't throw stones means that we shouldn't judge or criticize other people if we have faults. (People who live in glass houses shouldn't walk around naked either!)

If you are *as snug as a bug in a rug* you are cozy and comfortable.

I'm sure your grandma says
some special things, too.

Use this page to write the things
your grandma says to you!

Denise Brennan-Nelson

In 1999 Denise's first children's book, **Buzzy the bumblebee**, was published. She has been *busy as a bee* ever since. In addition to writing for children, Denise travels around the country giving workshops and presentations to students, teachers, parents, and businesses.

Denise thinks her husband Bob is the *bee's knees*, *cat's pajamas*, and *cream of the crop*. They have two daughters, Rebecca and Rachel, who only get up *on the wrong side of the bed once in a blue moon*. According to them, their mom is as *cool as a cucumber…* when she's not *running around like a chicken with her head cut off*.

Home sweet home for Denise and her family is in Howell, Michigan.

Jane Monroe Donovan

Jane is as *happy as a clam* when she is painting and the *proof is in the pudding*. She calls her painting a *labor of love*. She always *goes the extra mile* and would like to author and illustrate children's books *'til the cows come home*.

Jane and Denise also know that two heads are better than one and have collaborated on **My Momma Likes to Say** and **My Teacher Likes to Say**. Jane is also the illustrator of **Black Beauty's Early Days in the Meadow**, and author and illustrator of the holiday favorite **Winter's Gift**.

Jane fell for her husband Bruce *hook, line, and sinker* when she was in high school and her two sons, Ryan and Joey, are the *apple of her eye*. *Home sweet home* for Jane is in Pinckney, Michigan.